MA.

INSPIRATIONAL LIVES

LANCE ARMSTRONG
RACING HERO

Peter Hicks

WAYLAND

First published in 2010 by Wayland

Copyright © Wayland 2010

Wayland
338 Euston Road
London NW1 3BH

Wayland Australia
Level 17/207 Kent Street
Sydney, NSW 2000

Senior editor: Camilla Lloyd
Designer: Rob Walster
Picture researcher: Shelley Noronha

Acknowledgements: p.14 Inspiration: *It's Not About the Bike* by Lance Armstrong.

Picture acknowledgments: The author and publisher would like to thank the following for allowing their pictures to be reproduced in this publication: Cover: © Pascal Pavani/AFP/Getty Images; © Jean-Yves Rusniewski/TempSport/Corbis: 15; © Elizabeth Kreutz/Corbis: 16, 17; © Bob Daemmrich/Corbis: 22; © Sergio Perez/Reuters/Corbis: 24; © Erich Schlegel/Corbis:28; © Wolfgang Rattay/Reuters/Corbis: 29; © Getty Images: 12; © Anja Niedringhaus/AFP/Getty Images: 13; © Chris Cole/Allsport/Getty Images: 14; © Keith Bedford/Getty Images: 25; © Linda Armstrong Kelly/Sports Illustrated/Getty Images: 6, 7, 9, 11, 18, 19, 20; © Patrick Kovarik/AFP/Getty Images: 5; © Pascal Pavani/AFP/Getty Images: 26; © Stephen Dunn/Getty Images: 8, 10;© Rex Features: 4, 21, 23, 27.

British Library Cataloguing in Publication Data:
Hicks, Peter, 1952-
Lance Armstrong. - (Inspirational lives)
1. Armstrong, Lance-Juvenile literature. 2. Cyclists- United States-Biography-Juvenile literature. 3. Bicycle racing-Juvenile literature.
I. Title II. Series
796.6'2'092-dc22

ISBN: 978 0 7502 6269 9

Printed in China

Wayland is a division of Hachette Children's Books, an Hachette UK company.

www.hachette.co.uk

Contents

The yellow jersey

In the summer of 1999, the 28-year-old road racing cyclist Lance Armstrong was at the peak of his physical fitness. A member of the US Postal team, his training was highly disciplined and he followed a strictly controlled diet. On 3 July Lance's fitness was put to the test at the start of the world's most famous and toughest road race, the Tour de France.

The yellow jersey is awarded to the rider with the quickest overall time.

WOW!

Lance's Texan friends pronounced 'maillot jaune' as 'mellow johnny.' It stuck, and Mellow Johnny is Lance's nickname!

The 'Tour' is a stage race, held over three weeks and consisting of 22 stages or legs of varying distances. The race around France has a maximum total distance of 4,000 kilometres and always has some difficult mountain stages in the **Alps** and **Pyrenees**.

For Lance, the race began well. In the first stage – the Prologue – a short time trial where all the competitors cycle individually over an 8-kilometre course, he hit the front with a winning time of 8 minutes and 2 seconds. This entitled him to wear the famous 'maillot jaune' or yellow jersey to show he was race leader.

Crucial to holding on to the jersey were his US Postal team-mates. On the flat, exposed and windswept roads they would form a protective shield around him. They also had to look out for other riders in the main group or **peleton**, crashes and over-enthusiastic spectators and photographers!

Lance built up an impressive lead over the other riders and when the race ended in

As Lance rode his victory lap, a stranger gave him the American flag to raise.

Paris he was 7 minutes and 37 seconds ahead of the next rider. He'd won his first yellow jersey.

The extraordinary thing about his victory is that only two years before, Lance had been desperately fighting cancer!

INSPIRATION

"Strength does not come from physical capacity. It comes from an indomitable (unbeatable) will." Mahatma Gandhi

Growing up in Texas

Lance Armstrong was born Lance Edward Gunderson on 18 September 1971, in Dallas, Texas, USA. His mother was Linda Mooneyham and his father Eddie Gunderson. Linda was only 17 when she had Lance and was fiercely proud of her son. The couple separated before Lance was two and he has never met nor had any contact with his father.

TOP TIP

"Make every obstacle an opportunity. Make a negative a positive."
Linda Mooneyham

Lance celebrates his fifth birthday!

Life was tough for single mum Linda and Lance living in a small flat. Finishing school and working part-time she earned $400 a month but rent and childcare cost her $300. She always tried to provide little luxuries and Lance remembers being taken to the nearby store and treated to an ice-cold slurpee!

INSPIRATION

Lance admits he owes everything to his Mum, Linda. Her strength, willpower, resourcefulness and kindness taught him important lessons when he was growing up.

When Linda got a job as a secretary life improved a little. They moved to a nicer flat in a suburb of north Dallas called Richardson. On their weekly trip to the doughnut store they always passed the Richardson Bike Mart, which was a bike shop. The owner, who was looking for racers to **sponsor** on his bikes, worked out a deal with Linda for Lance's first proper bike.

When Lance was three, Linda re-married. His new stepfather was Terry Armstrong who officially adopted Lance in 1974. Lance and Terry had a very difficult relationship. Whenever Lance did anything wrong like coming home late or leaving his room untidy Terry was physically very strict. Not surprisingly, Lance had no affection for his stepfather.

When he was 14, Linda told Lance she was divorcing Terry. Lance recalls that after this he became much closer to his mother and she was much happier and more relaxed.

Lance loved his bike even though he described it as "an ugly brown with yellow wheels."

IronKid!

When Lance was about 11, he realised that he wasn't very good at American football. In Plano where he lived everyone loved football. Lance decided to try other sports he could be successful in. Lance was a good runner, winning a distance race in 5th Grade at his primary school.

WOW!

As a 12 year-old, Lance's swimming training was intensive. He swam 10 kilometres (km) a day and cycled a 32-km round trip to the pool!

Seventeen-year-old Lance putting on his wetsuit in preparation for the swimming leg of a *triathlon* in May 1988.

He also joined a swimming club, but was so bad at first that the instructor put him in a group with seven-year-olds! However, with good coaching and **dedication** he became a highly competent swimmer. At 12, he was fourth in the state of Texas at the 1,500-metre freestyle.

One day in 1983, Lance was in the bike shop when a poster for a local competition called IronKids caught his eye. IronKids was a junior triathlon, which contained all his best sports – swimming, running and cycling. On the spur of the moment he entered. His Mum kitted him out in a triathlon outfit and complete with his first racing bike, he tried his luck. Lance won by a very large margin. This victory was followed by another in Houston in 1984. Soon he was the best triathlete in his age group in Texas.

Lance entered as many races as possible, even pretending to be older and competing with the seniors.

Lance with his Mother, Linda. She has given him great support throughout his career.

INSPIRATION

The night before his first running race, his Mum gave him a 1972 silver dollar and told him "This is a good-luck coin...all you have to do is beat that clock". He won.

At 15, he entered an adult event – the 1987 President's Triathlon in Lake Levon, Texas and caused a stir by coming 32nd. People could not believe such a young competitor could do so well. The next year he came 5th!

Cycling versus school

Although Lance was an exceptional triathlete – by 16 he was earning $20,000 a year – he experienced a great deal of **snobbery** at Plano High School. There was pressure to wear designer labels and to fit in with the popular set. Lance and his Mum could not compete because they focused their time and energy on his training.

WOW!

Six days before a triathlon, a car knocked Lance off his bike. He was concussed and needed stitches. The doctor told him not to compete or do anything for three weeks. Lance ignored the advice and came 3rd.

Lance on the running leg of the Jeep Triathlon Grand Prix in May 1988.

HONOURS BOARD

Triathlon Successes:
1985 – 2nd IronKids National Championship
1987 – Texas State Triathlon Champion
1988 – Athens (Texas) YMCA Triathlon Champion (Course Record)
1989 – US National Sprint Triathlon Champion (Waco, Texas)
1990 – US National Sprint Triathlon Champion (McKinney, Texas)
1991 – Challenge of Champions Triathlon (Monterey, California)

Lance felt like an outsider. Some of his friends said disapprovingly, "If I were you, I'd be embarrassed to wear those lycra shorts." He reflected that while his school friends drove cars their parents bought them his car was paid for with his own hard-earned cash.

Lance was becoming incredibly fit because of his longer training rides. After camping in Texoma, his friends were picked up by their parents. He rode the nearly 100 km home on his own!

During his last year at High School, Lance came into conflict with the school authorities. He had been chosen to represent America in the 1990 Junior World Cycling championships in Moscow. With training he would be away for six weeks, but the school did not allow unexcused absences. Lance went, but on return faced zero grades and impossible catch-up targets for his subjects. His ever-**resourceful** Mum got him into a private school so he could graduate on time.

Lance with fellow triathlete and coach, Mark Allen in 1987.

Turning professional

When Lance was 18 he was chosen for the US national cycling team and left home to train and compete in Europe. It was very exciting, but he soon found out he had a lot to learn. As the US team manager Chris Carmichael realised, Lance was a very strong racer but had no idea about the tactics needed to win a race.

TOP TIP

"What makes a great **endurance** athlete is the ability to absorb potential embarrassment and to suffer without complaint."
Lance Armstrong

Lance in his Motorola cap, after winning the 7th Stage of the Tour du Pont in Beech, North Carolina.

In his first big international race, the 1990 Amateur World Championship in Japan, Lance was told to hang back and avoid the front. Instead, he opened up a 45-second lead only to be caught on the steep hills, finishing 11th. It was the best ever performance by an American, but Chris Carmichael told him "If you'd conserved your energy, you'd have been in the medals."

Lance finished a very respectable 14th in the Barcelona Olympics in 1992 and turned professional, riding for the Motorola team. Things started badly. In freezing cold rain he came last out of 111 riders in the San Sebastian Classic in Spain. He considered giving up, but remembered his Mum's encouraging words: "Never quit!" Two days later he came 2nd in the Championship of Zurich. Gradually, Lance learned where he was going wrong. He listened to his trainers and realised that he had to save his energy for when he needed it.

In 1993 Lance enjoyed great success. He won $1 million for the Thrift Drug Triple Crown (winning three US races) and became the World Cycling Champion in Oslo in torrential rain!

WOW!

Before meeting King Harald of Norway after becoming World Champion, Lance was told his Mum would have to stay outside. "Come on, let's go," he said and started to leave. Security relented and the audience took place with the champion's Mum!

Lance is elated after winning the Thrift Drug Triple Crown in 1993.

The tragic Tour

During the 1995 Tour de France, one of Lance's favourite Motorola team-mates was the Italian Olympic Champion, Fabio Casartelli. Fabio was a fine young rider, newly married with a month-old baby. On Stage 15, while on a dangerous **descent** he crashed and hit a concrete barrier. Fabio was airlifted to hospital in Tarbes, southwest France, but died soon after arrival.

INSPIRATION

"I learned what it means to ride the Tour de France. It's not about the bike. It's a **metaphor** for life. It is a test. It tests you physically, it tests you mentally and it even tests you morally... I understand that now."
Lance Armstrong

Fabio competed against Lance in the 1992 Barcelona Olympics. Fabio won the gold.

The death of this talented and popular rider devastated the team. Half of the riders wanted to stop and go home, while the other half wanted to keep riding. They were visited by Fabio's wife, Annalisa, who asked them to carry on because she was sure Fabio would have wanted them to. The next day, Stage 16 was a memorial to Fabio and all the riders stopped to allow the Motorola team to cross the line together. His bike was mounted on the team car with a black ribbon.

WOW!

All professional cyclists have to have random drug tests. They are asked to provide urine and blood samples. This is unwelcome but necessary in the fight against the use of drugs in sport.

When the team learned that Fabio had wanted to win the Limoges Stage (18), Lance wanted to win it for him. Twenty-five miles from the finish and on a downhill stretch, Lance shocked the leaders with a sudden breakaway. He opened up a 30-second gap, then 45 seconds! As he crossed the line a minute ahead of the next riders, Lance pointed his fingers to the sky and looked heavenward. This experience had a massive impact on the young Lance Armstrong. It helped him grow up.

Three dates are listed on Fabio's memorial: his birthday, the day he won an Olympic Gold in 1992 and his tragic death.

A day in the life of Lance Armstrong

Lance's day begins at 7 am when he likes to get up, make coffee and read the papers. If anything interrupts this routine he might become grumpy!

By 9 am he has checked his e-mails and dealt with messages concerning his foundation Livestrong, which works to unite cancer sufferers and campaigns for better treatment. For breakfast Lance has fruit or muesli, then egg whites and bread. Most days he tries to eat with his children and help them get ready for school.

Lance has converted his garage into a small gym where he can work out.

TOP TIP

Lance constantly trains. Lance has said: "If you ask me when I should be preparing for the next Tour, my answer was, 'the morning after.'"

Most of his training takes place on the bike. A daily ride varies from three to seven hours. On the shorter rides he will train alone, but for the longer ones he has a friend on a motorbike to protect him from traffic. When he's finished training he goes home, showers, eats a pasta meal, deals with his phone calls and e-mails and then takes a well-earned nap.

When Lance wakes he has a family dinner – fish or chicken with steamed vegetables – and then he might play football with his children in the garden. They watch television, Lance loves watching American football and the children go to bed. He reads or watches more television before going to bed at about 10 pm.

Lance loves rock music and likes going to concerts. Lance recently saw Pearl Jam, Wilco and U2 live in concert.

Lance's friend and coach, Chris Carmichael paces and protects him on a training ride in Hawaii.

During training Lance will ride hundreds of kilometres between 30 and 65 km/h, lose 10–12 litres of fluid and burn at least 6,000 calories!

Cancer

Throughout 1995–6, Lance's cycling was going really well and he felt at the height of his career. However, in the summer of 1996, things began to go wrong. Due to illness, he dropped out of the Tour de France after only five days and only finished 12th in the Atlanta Olympics.

WOW!

When Lance was diagnosed with cancer he asked Dr. Reeves what his chances of survival were. He was told 50%, but his doctor later admitted he privately thought it was only 20%.

Lance having blood taken just before his brain operation. The dots on his head were to guide the surgeon.

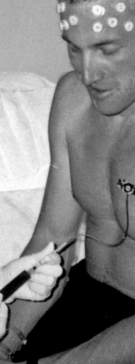

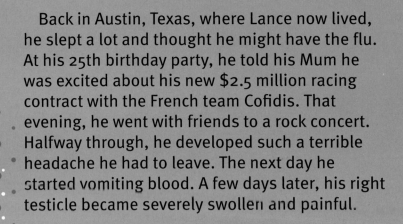

Back in Austin, Texas, where Lance now lived, he slept a lot and thought he might have the flu. At his 25th birthday party, he told his Mum he was excited about his new $2.5 million racing contract with the French team Cofidis. That evening, he went with friends to a rock concert. Halfway through, he developed such a terrible headache he had to leave. The next day he started vomiting blood. A few days later, his right testicle became severely swollen and painful.

Lance's friend and doctor, Rick Parker arranged for an immediate hospital appointment. On 2 October, after a series of tests, the specialist, Dr. Jim Reeves told Lance that he had advanced testicular cancer and it had spread to his lungs. This was a terrible shock and a devastating blow. Lance was scared and convinced his cycling career was over. Dr. Reeves told him he would need to have immediate surgery to remove the testicle and start **chemotherapy**. After this treatment began, Lance received another blow. He was told the cancer had spread to his brain.

Lance sought advice from a team of specialists in Indianapolis, Dr. Craig Nicholls and surgeon Scott Shapiro. Lance was not sure about them at first, but they won him over and the operation on his brain was a complete success. The cancer cells were found to be dying and safely removed.

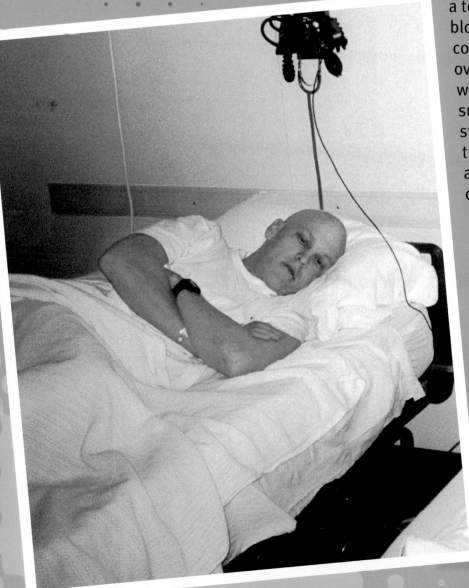

Lance in the middle of his aggressive cancer treatment.

Treatment and recovery

Lance's survival now depended on his course of chemotherapy. The course involves being fed **intravenously** very powerful chemicals that kill cancer cells. The side effects are terrible. Patients lose their hair, become pale and lose muscle weight. Even worse symptoms are the vomiting, pains and feelings of total weakness.

Lance had four cycles of treatment in a period of three months and he suffered badly. His gums bled and he had terrible sores in his mouth. He lost his appetite and the only food he could tolerate were apple fritters, brought to him every day by his old Motorola manger Jim Ochowicz.

A welcome visit from Belgian cycling legend, Eddy Merckx. Eddy is a five-time winner of the Tour de France.

In between treatments, Lance went home to recover. He refused the wheelchair that was sent to carry him to the hospital entrance: "No way, I'm walking out of here," he angrily told staff. He was afraid his body was weakening and desperately wanted to keep active. At home, he went on bike rides with his friends. Dr. Nicholls told him not to stress his body. His **oncology** nurse, LaTrice Haney told him, "listen to your body, let it rest."

One of the bleakest moments of his treatment came when his French sponsor, Cofidis, visited Lance in hospital and told his agent that his contract was under threat because of his illness. He could not believe their bad timing and Lance was hurt that they thought he might not survive. His last chemotherapy treatment was on 13 December 1996. The wait to see if he was cured was unbearable.

WOW!

Lance realised how weak he was when on one of his rides he was overtaken by a 50-year-old woman!

INSPIRATION

"There are angels on this earth and ... I decided LaTrice Haney was one of them." He asked her why she was a cancer nurse and she replied: "My satisfaction is to make it a little easier for people."

Lance, back at home in Austin, Texas in between his chemotherapy treatments.

The comeback

After Lance left hospital he went home to consider what direction his life should take. However, he was convinced that he should start a cancer **foundation** to raise awareness of the fact 8 million Americans suffered from the disease. He decided to organise a sponsored bike ride called Ride for the Roses in March 1997.

Lance leading a pack of elite riders in the 2003 Ride for the Roses.

The ride was a great success and raised over $200,000 for the foundation. While working on the event, Lance met Kristin Richard. They got to know each other well and went to Europe together in the summer. Lance had to appear at the Tour de France for his sponsors, so he delighted in showing Kristin all the colourful excitement of the world's greatest bike race. They fell in love and married in May 1998.

Lance was still weak and had nightmares in which his cancer returned. If ever he caught a cold or infection he was afraid his cancer had come back. He thought his cycling career was over.

However, by the end of the summer he felt better. His hair grew back and he felt good on his bike. On 4 September 1997, Lance announced he would return to competitive cycling for the 1998 season. He left Cofidis and signed for the new US Postal team. In October, his doctors told him officially that he had almost certainly beaten cancer.

Lance at a book signing of his 2003 bestseller Every Second Counts.

Unfortunately, his comeback in 1998 started disastrously. Lance dropped out of the cold, wet and windy Paris to Nice race and he swore he would never compete again. He and Kristin returned to Austin where he relaxed and played lots of golf.

TOP TIP

'Carpe Diem' – Latin for 'seize the day'. It's one of Lance's favourite sayings and means live every day as if it was your last.

Turning point

Lance's old friend and manager Chris Carmichael flew into Austin and tried to persuade him to get fit. Chris suggested leaving Austin because of its many distractions. Lance said he would like to go to Boone in North Carolina, a town high in the Appalachian Mountains. He loved the area and had twice won the Tour Du Pont there. So in April 1998 he and Chris rented a cabin there for 10 days.

Lance achieved the third fastest time in the individual time trial in the Tour of Spain, September 1998.

INSPIRATION

"You will look great on the **podium** of the Tour de France next year". E-mail to Lance from the US Postal team director, Johan Bruyneel.

In those 10 days, Lance's whole attitude changed. He enjoyed the air, the scenery, the food and the company. Most of all, he learned to love his bike again. On one training ride over Beech Mountain – a 1,500-metre climb, complete with snow-covered **summit** – Lance felt like his old self. He realised, during the difficult ascent that this was what his life was all about. He was born to race bikes and he understood he was well again. After the training camp at Boone, he never again thought about leaving the sport.

In June, he came 4th in the US Pro Championships and then him and Kristen returned to Europe. They rented a flat in Nice in the south of France and Lance found some success. He won the 4-day tour of Luxembourg and came 4th in both the Tours of Holland and Spain. In the Tour of Spain he only missed third place by 6 seconds and was only 2 minutes and 18 seconds behind the winner.

The 1998 season had started badly for Lance, but by the time he returned to Austin that autumn, he was brimming with confidence. What would 1999 hold in store for him?

Lance and Kristen attend the 2002 SportsMan of the Year Awards. Sadly, they divorced in 2003.

HONOURS BOARD

Awards Lance has won:
United States Olympic Committee SportsMan of the Year, 1999, 2001, 2002, 2003
World's most Outstanding Athlete Award, 2000
Reuters Sportsman of the Year, 2003

Record breaker

Lance's 1999 Tour de France victory caused a sensation. Lance had just won the world's greatest cycle race, but only two-and-a-half years earlier he was battling for his life against advanced cancer. It was a special time for Lance because in October, Kristin gave birth to a baby boy, Luke. Lance would have to adapt to being a parent as well as a cycling superstar.

WOW!

Traditionally, the Tour winner splits the $400,000 prize money with his team-mates. In 2002, Lance doubled the amount as a thank you to his US Postal team!

Lance powering towards the finish of the individual time trial in the Tour de France, 2009.

26

Lance was determined to win the 2000 Tour de France. He was annoyed because his previous victory had been called a fluke by some commentators because some of the big names had not taken part. In 2000, two former winners returned to the race, Jan Ullrich and Marco Pantani, so Lance knew he was in for a tough race.

Things went well for Lance and he built up a healthy lead but on stage 16 he made a terrible mistake. He had not eaten enough and ascending Joux-Plane, a very tough climb, experienced a **'hunger flat'**. Suddenly Lance felt he was going backwards and lost all power in his legs. He could easily lose his time lead. Luckily, and totally unselfishly, two riders Roberto Conti and Guido Trentin helped get him up. They shielded him from the wind until the summit and then Lance freewheeled down losing only 97 seconds from his lead. A few days later when he climbed the podium to take his second yellow jersey, Kristin and Luke were there to greet him.

Incredibly, Lance went on to win the next five Tours to become the record holder for the largest number of wins. After winning the centenary Tour in 2003 he joined an exclusive group of only four riders who had won it five times. After wins in 2004 and 2005 his record stands at seven consecutive victories!

HONOURS BOARD

Tour de France victories:

1999 (4 stage wins)
2000 (1 stage win)
2001 (4 stage wins)
2002 (4 stage wins)
2003 (1 stage win)
2004 (5 stage wins)
2005 (1 stage win)

Kristin hands Lance his son, Luke, during the Tour de France's winners' ceremony in 2000.

The impact of Lance Armstrong

Lance is on record as saying that if he had to choose between winning the Tour de France or getting cancer, he'd choose cancer. This incredible statement needs some explanation. He feels that he was lucky to get cancer because it made him who he is now. He was tested by the illness and it ended up making him a better person. Having survived, he feels that it is now his responsibility to campaign for the nine million Americans who have survived cancer.

TOP TIP

Lance believes that it is worth leaving your **comfort zone** in life otherwise you never know what you can achieve.

Lance is thoughtful at the start of the 2008 Livestrong Challenge in Texas.

Lance's foundation is called Livestrong and it raises funds to improve the quality of life for survivors of cancer and those who are struggling with the disease. Since the first Ride for the Roses in 1997 the foundation has raised many millions of dollars to educate, inform, train, research and campaign for a better understanding of cancer and cancer survivorship. Lance Is not religious but he firmly believes it was his destiny to be a champion for cancer sufferers. As one of the most famous athletes in the world he can use his reputation to raise Livestrong's profile. In 2009, Lance came out of a four-year retirement to compete in the Tour de France. At 37, he still showed fighting qualities and gained 3rd place on the podium.

In August, Lance rode in the Tour of Ireland and was in Glasgow a few days before to see a U2 concert. Lance sent out a 'Twitter': "Glasgow, Scotland!! I'm coming your way tomorrow. Who wants to go for a bike ride??" Hundreds turned up for a chance to meet a living legend. He also announced in the summer that he will ride in the 2010 Tour de France for his new RadioShack team. Lance continues to be an inspiration for millions of people worldwide.

WOW!

When Lance ran the 2006 New York Marathon in just under 3 hours – a highly respectable time – he raised $600,000 for Livestrong.

Lance takes the 17th stage of the Tour de France in 2004.

Have you got what it takes to be an endurance athlete? Try this!

1) Do you like spending your spare time out of doors in all weathers?
a) Yes, I prefer the outdoors.
b) I like the outdoors, but not when it's cold and wet!
c) No, I prefer being indoors.

2) Have you got a high boredom threshold to cope with long hours of training?
a) Yes, I can usually stick at most things.
b) Yes, but I would need breaks.
c) No, I get very easily bored.

3) Are you prepared to sacrifice a 'normal' social life to achieve peak fitness?
a) Yes, it would not bother me.
b) I would be prepared to cut back on my social life a bit.
c) No, my social life is the most important thing for me.

4) Can you cope with high levels of pain during training and events?
a) Pain isn't nice, but I'd put up with it to achieve a goal.
b) I think I would find it a challenge!
c) No! I don't do pain.

5) Can you stick to a diet that might not include your favourite foods?
a) Yes, because you need to eat properly to help your performance.
b) Probably, but I'd miss certain foods.
c) No, I am very 'picky' when it comes to my food!

7) Have you the self-discipline to train for long periods of time on your own?
a) Yes, I could always listen to my iPod (if it was safe!).
b) I tend to like doing things with other people, but for short periods.
c) No, I like doing things in a group or crowd.

RESULTS

Mostly As: It appears that you are totally cut out for endurance events. Join that cycling, swimming, athletic or rowing club now!

Mostly Bs: You have a healthy interest in sport. Perhaps you could start with more gentle, rather than endurance, events!

Mostly Cs: Time to ditch the television and computer and get fit!

Glossary

Alps A high mountain range in southern Europe that the Tour de France passes through.

chemotherapy Treatment of cancer by powerful chemicals that attack cancerous cells.

comfort zone A place in which you feel safe and comfortable, but your abilities and strengths are not tested.

dedication When you give the maximum time and effort to achieve something.

descent A steep climb down a hill or a mountain.

endurance The ability to keep going during difficult, unpleasant and painful experiences.

foundation An organisation that raises money for a particular charity.

hunger flat When an athlete experiences great weakness because of lack of food and water.

intravenously When drugs or food are injected directly into a vein.

metaphor An expression which describes something by referring to something else which is similar, for example the challenges of the Tour de France are the challenges of life.

oncology The treatment and the study of cancer.

peleton The main group or bulk of riders in the Tour de France.

podium A raised platform where winners receive their medals or prizes.

Pyrenees A high mountain range on the French-Spanish border.

resourceful The ability to have the ideas and the strength to overcome difficulties or problems.

snobbery The act of only liking or respecting people of a high social class.

sponsor To support a person by providing them with money or equipment.

summit The peak or top of a mountain.

triathlon An endurance event involving swimming, running and cycling long distances.

Index

INSPIRATIONAL LIVES

Contents of titles in series:

Barack Obama
978 0 7502 6089 3

Inauguration
Barack's family
Life in Indonesia
School and college
The world of work
Law school success
A day in the life of Barack Obama
Lawyer, husband, teacher and writer
The political life
Senator Obama
Winning the democratic nomination
The 2008 presidential election
The impact of Barack Obama
Have you got what it takes to be a politician?

Jamie Oliver
978 0 7502 6268 2

Cooking up a storm
The young tearaway
Tinkering in the kitchen
London calling
The big break
The Naked Chef
A day in the life of Jamie Oliver
Oliver's Twist
Charity begins in the kitchen
Food fights
Jamie conquers America
A quiet celebrity
The impact of Jamie Oliver
Have you got what it takes to be a top chef?

J.K. Rowling
978 0 7502 6273 6

A flash of inspiration
An imaginative child
Town and countryside in Tutshill
Teenage years
A secretary's story
Life in Portugal
A day in the life of J.K.Rowling

Difficult times
Harry Potter and the Philosopher's Stone
Catapulted
to fame
Harry on the big screen
A quiet celebrity
The impact of J.K.Rowling
Have you got what it takes to be a fiction writer?

Lance Armstrong
978 0 7502 6269 9

The yellow jersey
Growing up in Texas
IronKid!
Cycling versus school
Turning professional
The tragic Tour
A day in the life of Lance Armstrong
Cancer
Treatment and recovery
The comeback
Turning point
Record breaker
The impact of Lance Armstrong
Have you got what it takes to be an endurance athlete?

Richard Branson
978 0 7502 6271 2

The daredevil business man
Childhood challenges
School days
The accidental entrepreneur
Virgin in born
Recording in the countryside
A day in the life of Richard Branson
Virgin takes to the skies
The publicity machine
Mind the gap!
Changing the world
The final frontier
The impact of Richard Branson
Have you got what it takes to be an entrepreneur?

Simon Cowell
978 0 7502 6272 9

The birth of TV's Mr Nasty
The early days
Simon's school days
Starting at the bottom
Budding entrepreneur
Wrestlers and Westlife
A day in the life of Simon Cowell
Pop Idol Mania
Breaking America
The X Factor
Simon's got talent
From Mr Nasty to TV's hero
The impact of Simon Cowell
Have you got what it takes to be a music mogul?

The Beckhams
978 0 7502 6270 5

Together forever, eternally
Meet the families
Childhood
High kicks and kick offs
Spice up your life
Posh and Becks
A day in the life of the Beckhams
The football legend
Making the right moves
All for a good cause
California dreaming
Fashion, footy and beyond
The impact of the Beckhams
Have you got what it takes to be like the Beckhams?